DATE DUE

MAY

Big Machines At Work

Dump Trucks

By Jean Eick

The Child's World® Inc. ◆ Eden Prairie, Minnesota

Published by The Child's World®, Inc.
7081 W. 192 Ave.
Eden Prairie, MN 55346

Designed and Production:
The Creative Spark, San Juan Capistrano, CA.

Photos: © 1998 David M. Budd Photography

Library of Congress Cataloging-in-Publication Data
Eick, Jean, 1947-
        Dump Trucks at work / by Jean Eick.
            p. cm.
        Includes Index.
        Summary: Briefly describes the parts of a dump truck and how it works.
        ISBN 1-56766-526-8 (library reinforced : alk. paper)
        1. Dump trucks--Juvenile literature. 2. Earthmoving machinery--Juvenile literature. [1.
Dump trucks.] I. Title.
TA439.E33 1998
732.1'52--dc21
                                                                        98-3134
                                                                          CIP
                                                                           AC

Contents

On the Job

On the job, dump trucks work at
construction sites. They carry heavy
loads of dirt for the workers.

The big box on the back of this dump

truck is being filled by a front-end loader.

Sometimes the truck bounces as the

huge load crashes into the box!

Soon the box is full. Now the truck

takes the load to the place where it is

to be dumped.

Beep, beep!

The truck backs up and stops.

Up, up goes the heavy box. Long arms
push the box up.

These arms are called **hoists**. Quickly

the dirt falls to the ground!

Bang! The box drops down. Off goes the dump truck to pick up another load.

Climb Aboard!

Would you like to see where the driver sits? Climb aboard! The dump truck's driver is called the **operator**. The operator uses a stick called a **lever** to make the hoists lift the box.

The big mirrors on the side help the

operator see where to back up.

Up Close

1. The cab

2. The hoists

3. The box

4. The levers

Glossary

hoists (HOYSTS)

Hoists are the arms that lift the box of the dump truck. They hold the box up until the dirt falls out.

lever (LEV-er)

A dump truck's lever is a stick with a round knob on the end. It is used to raise the hoists.

operator (OP-er-ay-tur)

The operator is the person who drives the dump truck and makes it work.